How to Build a Website

(For Beginners)

Create and Promote your Dream Website

By John Gower III

Disclaimer:
Although the author and publisher have made every effort to ensure that the information in this book was correct at press time, the author and publisher do not assume and hereby disclaim any liability to any party for any loss, damage, or disruption caused by errors or omissions, whether such errors or omissions result from negligence, accident, or any other cause.

ISBN: 1466327782

ISBN 13: 9781466327788 (Paperback)

Table of Contents

PART III: GETTING YOUR SITE OUT THERE

Introduction

In this, book, titled "How to Build a Website (For Beginners)" by John Gower III, will layout step-by-step instructions on website building for beginners. It will be very easy systematic simple instructions. In addition, this book will teach you how to build a website in an easy new fast effective way.

PART I
PLAN FIRST

CHAPTER 1

Learning about Websites

Building your own website can be easy, other people look at it as a hard and complicated thing to do when you finish with this book you will know how to build your own website. This book will explain the basic steps on how you can build your own website free. Now you can build your dream website for your business or personal use. This book will show you how to do it all!

There are many ways that you can build a website using HTML, Java, FrontPage, Dreamweaver and many other programs. This book titled "How to Build a Website (for Beginners)" by John Gower III will teach you a new way to build a website for free, easier and faster way to publish your URL at low cost annually to you.

In this book, you will learn how to build a website through an online site called webs. It is very easy, simple, and free.

In this book, I will explain to you as simple as possible for you to understand the concepts of this book.

To help you understand how to build a basic five-page website, buy a domain name, and have a published domain name on the internet.

In addition, you will also learn how to submit your site into the search engines. Therefore, you will be able to see your URL name in the search sites like Google, Bing and Yahoo.

What you need before you start;

1) basic computer skills

2) access to a computer

3) access to the internet

4) a webs.com account

5) a email address

6) a domain name

The first step in the building process is preparing and planning your site before you start building.

Of course, it is easy to build a website. However, it has to make sense. You must get your point across to people.

This is why you want to first. Brainstorm for ideas; get a blank sheet of paper out with a pencil. Sit and think on what you want your website to be.

Some ideas you can work with to help you get started as you brainstorm.

You can choose to make an online E-Commerce store for your business, which allows people to shop on your website you can sell your products right from your site or you can choose to make your own personal website for friends to blog with friends and fans, and family.

There is no limit to what you can make your website about just open your mind and use your imagination.

In this book, there will be systematic instructions on how to build a basic simple web site using the online site builder from webs. http://www.webs.com .

There are other methods as well that you can use to build your website such as; HTML, Dreamweaver, FrontPage, but they are more time consuming.

However, each step and example in this book will teach you an easier and quicker way to build and publish a website in less time.

Let us get started, in the example website I am going to build as I write this book. It will be a simple 5-page site. It will have a sub domain instead of a regular published domain.

However, your site will have a domain name when you finish this book. The difference between domain names is it has a .com at the end of the URL and is available to the public.

Before you get started, put a bookmark in this page set the book down. Go take a break, then come back go to your computer that you have built from my other book titled "How to Build a Computer (For Beginners)" by John Gower III.

Open your internet browser up and in the address bar type in www.webs.com, and create and sign up for a webs account with your email address, once you finish signing up then continue reading.

To help you remember your username and password for your webs account. Write it in this book on page 14. This way if you ever forget your login you can always go back to this book as a reference.

Notes:

Username: _____

Password: _____

Your title of your website:

_____

Your domain name: _____

CHAPTER 2

Preparation

In this chapter, I will teach you how to construct your website on paper first.

Get a blank sheet of paper and a pencil. Write down the title of the site you want to have at the top of the paper.

In my site example, I am going to make a website titled, "My Fan Page". I will use this site for all my fans that buy and follow my books online.

You can make up any title you wish to have for your site.

OK, now we got the title, next is the home page introduction.

In example paragraph, 1-1 is a sample paragraph introduction for my homepage introduction.

1:1: "Welcome to my fan site. Please feel free to browse. Don't forget to sign up for free as a member on my website."

This should give you some insight on what you can have for an introduction for your home page. You may use any introduction for your home page for your website within certain standards.

Tip! (Try to make your introduction short simple and to the point.)

I will leave you space below to write your ideas for your website.

Write your ideas and your words here before you type them in to your website.

Define your objectives for your website:

_____

_____

_____

_____

_____

_____

_____

_____

_____

_____

Once you know exactly what you intend to do with your site and you know who the targeted audience will be, the next step is to determine the mood of your website. Should the ambience be informal, professional or high tech?

Do not forget that people use many different types of personal computers, modems and versions of software. A web page that loads quickly on your machine might not function quite as well on another. When writing web pages, the golden rule: small is the key. Once you have all the information written down you are ready for the next step.

PART II
TIME TO BUILD

CHAPTER 3

Constructing your Site

Please read the following steps carefully. Make sure you do not skip a step. Go to www.webs.com and log in to your webs account that you previously made in chapter 1.

Be careful when building your website you can very easily lose your work. So make sure always, save your work. [1] *(See example 1 on the following page)*

_____

[1] Tip: Make sure you are always save your work on every step that you make building your website. If you do not save it, you will lose your work progress. I will not be responsible for any data loss.

Step One: Logging In

Log in to your webs account as *(shown in example 1 below).* If you do not have an account, you must create one.

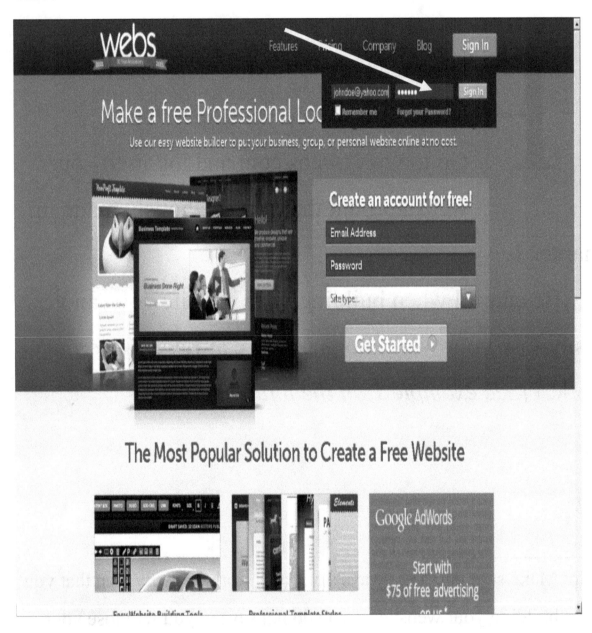

Step Two: Creating your Site

Put in your site address, displayed in the browser bar once created. It also will be the sub domain name for your site temporarily until you purchase your own domain name. *(In example 2, shows my example site name "fanpagesite".)*

Next put in your site title, this will be the title of your website site. It will also appear on the top of your webpage. *(See example 2, on page 27)*

In my example website, I am going to make the site title name, "My Fan Page".

Next, select a category. Select the category you chose with your title.

For my example website, I am going to choose the fan site category.

Next, select a template, there are many to choose. Take the time to browse through until you find the one you want for your site. This will be the theme for your website's background and text.

In example 2, there is a picture to help you see what to do. *(See example 2 on the following page)*

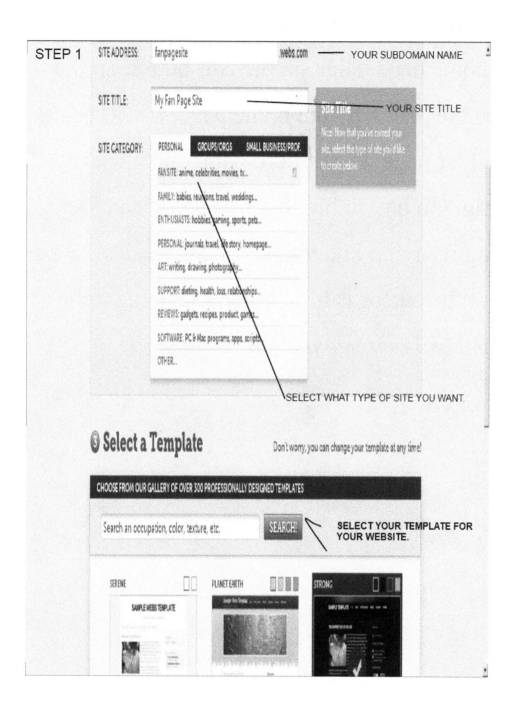

STEP 1

SITE ADDRESS: fanpagesite .webs.com ——— YOUR SUBDOMAIN NAME

SITE TITLE: My Fan Page Site ——— YOUR SITE TITLE

Site Title

Nice! Now that you've named your site, select the type of site you'd like to create below.

SITE CATEGORY: PERSONAL | GROUPS/ORGS | SMALL BUSINESS/PROF.

FAN SITE: anime, celebrities, movies, tv...

FAMILY: babies, reunions, travel, weddings...

ENTHUSIASTS: hobbies, gaming, sports, pets...

PERSONAL: journals, travel, life story, homepage...

ART: writing, drawing, photography...

SUPPORT: dieting, health, loss, relationships...

REVIEWS: gadgets, recipes, product, games...

SOFTWARE: PC & Mac programs, apps, scripts

OTHER...

SELECT WHAT TYPE OF SITE YOU WANT.

③ Select a Template   Don't worry, you can change your template at any time!

CHOOSE FROM OUR GALLERY OF OVER 300 PROFESSIONALLY DESIGNED TEMPLATES

Search an occupation, color, texture, etc. | SEARCH!   SELECT YOUR TEMPLATE FOR YOUR WEBSITE.

SERENE | PLANET EARTH | STRONG

SAMPLE WEBS TEMPLATE | Sample Webs Template | SAMPLE TEMPLATE

27

Step Three: Editing the Homepage

To edit your home page, click on the edit button on the where you see the pencil by the home page. It will bring up the site builder page. From there point and click to select the paragraph box to highlight it so you can see a cursor blinking if so you know that you are ready to type. Make sure that the cursor is blinking in the paragraph box. *(See example 3 on page the following page)*

Example

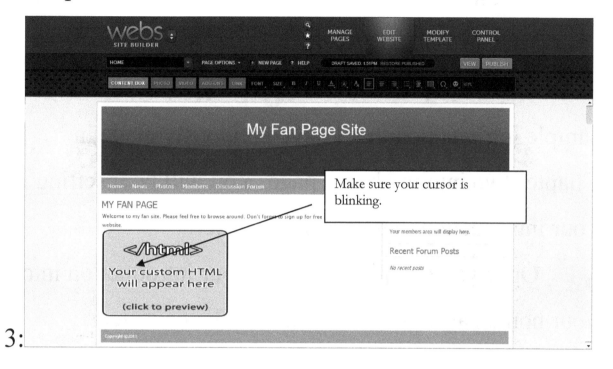

3:

Step Four: Writing your Introduction

In this step, you will type in your website introduction into the paragraph box on your home page. *(See example 3 on page 29)*

In my example website, I am going to type in my sample introduction that I have previously made in Chapter two into my home page. You will be inserting your introduction that you made earlier.

Once you completed typing your introduction into your home page, please continue to the next step.

Step Five: Inserting Photo(s)

In this step, you will learn how to insert pictures into your web page.

The first step in this process is click inside the content box where you wish to insert your photo(s).

It is very important to make sure the cursor is blinking in the box.

Now click the area on the page where you want to insert your photo(s). Then click the blue "PHOTO" button on your tool bar. *(Example 4 on the following page shows where the button is located.)*

The insert image box will appear. Click the "**Upload**" button in the center of the box. Locate on your computer a photo(s) you wish to upload. Once you find one select, it and it should then appear on your page.

You can also upload videos as well following the same procedure only change is you hit the blue "VIDEO" button on your tool bar. It is very important to save your work on everything you do.[2]

Example

4:

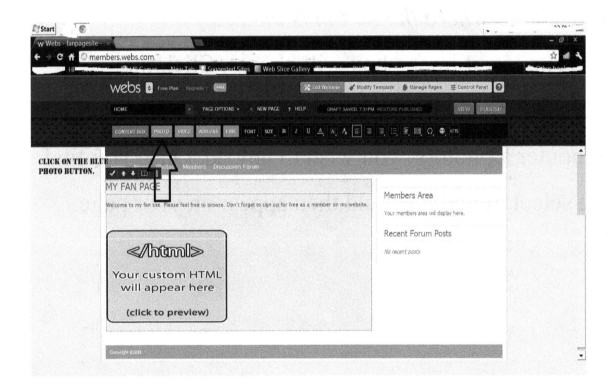

---

[2] **Important Note:** Make sure you hit the green "**Publish**" button each time you make changes to your web site. It saves your work so you do not lose your changes.

Step Six: Inserting Link(s)

In this step, you will be learning how to insert link(s) into your web page. The first step in this process is to, highlight the text you wish to link, and then click on the blue "LINK" button on your tool bars. You can choose multiple options.

You have the option to link to another website or you can link to your web pages. It also gives you the option to open in a new window or open the link in the existing page. *(See example 5 on the following page.)*

Example

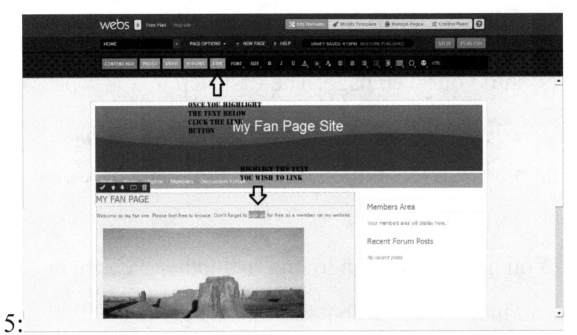

5:

Step Seven: Inserting Table(s)

Inserting a table into your web page is very simple and easy. First, choose an area on your web page you wish to insert your table. Then, on your web page click the table bar icon on your tool bar editor while logged in to webs site builder. Select how many rows and columns you wish to insert on the area you select in your site.

Step Eight: Inserting Video(s)

In this step, you will learn how to upload your own video in to your website. While logged in, click on the area in your page you wish to put a video into then click on the blue "VIDEO" tab on the tool bar you can upload your own video or you now have the options to upload a video from YouTube.

Step Nine: Customizing your Own Website

It is very simple to complete you site from here just experiment to get to know the tools and application on the site builder. You can make your website to what you want it to look.

In addition, you can work on it to your perfection. Take your time do not rush, and just take the knowledge that you learned from this book to figure out how you want site to look like.

If you have any questions or if you are stuck and have a question please go to my website http://www.jghitech.com. Log in to the fan club and email me personally if you have any questions.

If you did not join my fan club yet go to my site and click join my fan club and then create a profile. Then find me on the fan club page and email me.

CHAPTER 4

Previewing your Site

In this Chapter, you will preview what your website will look like to viewers. Go to your internet explorer and in the address bar type in the website address that you have created.

For example, my website name is http://www.myfansite.webs.com.

If you have already have purchased a domain name. Your site will have a .com ending not .webs.com ending to it. Once you get your domain name.

Your website should appear in your web browser. Go over and check to see if you want to make any additions or changes to your site.

Also, check and see if your links that you inserted to your homepage are working correctly, as you want them to.

PART III
GETTING YOUR SITE OUT THERE

CHAPTER 5

Purchasing a Domain Name

Purchasing a domain name can be tricky because there is many domains out there that you have in mind are probably taken already.

Go to the control panel on your webs.com site. Then look for Register for a Domain, once you select that you want see if a domain name is available read the instructions carefully because you only get one domain name. Register your domain name that you wish to use for your website by purchasing it for an annual rate.

Once finished then go to your browser and type in your domain name that you purchased into the address bar on your internet explorer.

Check and see if everything is working correctly. If it is then move on to chapter 6.

Write your domain name on the line below so you have it for future reference. _____

CHAPTER 6

Promoting Your Website

In this chapter, I will explain to you how to submit your website URL into search engines, like Google, Yahoo, and Bing. People around the world will be able to come across your website though the keywords on your site.

Many web page developers seem to think that if you build a page, people will come. Unfortunately, life is not quite so simple. With several billion pages on the Internet, the odds of someone bumping into yours is rather remote, unless well promoted.

Web page promotion entails registering your URL with one or more search engines and portals. There are literally hundreds of search engines in existence today.

Although it is free to add your URL to some search engines, the registration effort does take time. Most major search engines now charge fees for registration.

The first step in this task is to go to your internet web browser that you use. In the list below are examples of web site's you can go and submit your URL so that you can see your website in the search engines.

Sites You Can Submit Your URL:

https://www.google.com/webmasters/tools/submit-url?continue=/addurl&pli=1

https://ssl.bing.com/webmaster/SubmitSitePage.asp x

Once you submit your website to the search engines, it will take a couple days for it to show up into the search.

There is software that you can use to submit your site into a list of major searches. Look around in your local stores for them.

Promoting Your Website with Social Networking

How to promote your website though social networking to promote your website. The first step in this process you must:

1. Create a Facebook account if you do not have one already. Make sure you put your website in your profile page on Facebook so you can promote it.

2. Create a Twitter account if you do not have one already. Make sure you promote your URL in your profile.

3. Edit your profiles on all social media websites you use to include the URL to your website.

4. Promote your page to your personal Facebook network to attract more fans.

Make sure that you post links to your articles on your existing social networking sites. There is a fine line between posting useful information and spamming.

If you post links to everything you have done, whenever you do it, your links will lose meaning. These are your friends and they are clicking on the links because they know and trust you, not because they are incredibly interested in the subject.

Add buttons to your website that offers viewers the opportunity to post to your site on their social networks. If someone likes your site, the (person) s will post it on his or her social networking site. If enough of this happens then it will be like a domino effect and you will get an endless stream of social networking traffic.

CHAPTER 7

Conclusion

Congratulations! You should of by now have completed all the steps in chapter 5. You should have a complete finished website.

Just make sure you double-check your website for any mistakes. In addition, check all your links you put in and make sure they all work.

Once you are finished and everything seems to work right and look good. Contact the author of this book by going to his website: http://www.jghitech.com and send him an email and include the URL link to your website that you built using this book. Mention your name and at your request, he will link to your site on his links page on his website to help you get visitors on your newly published website.

About the Author

John Gower III was born in Philadelphia, Pennsylvania in 1985, where he grew up in the town of Brodheadsville raised by his mother and father. John attended Bangor Area High School, graduating in 2003. John attended college at Information Computer Systems Institute in Allentown, Pennsylvania, where he graduated with an associate's degree in Business/Data Networking in 2005. John now has ten years experience in computers working with software, hardware, networking, and web design.

John also has numerous certifications in the field of computers. John started writing books later on in his life. He published his first book on July 1, 2011 called, "How to Build a Computer (For Beginners)"©. John is currently still writing and publishing more educational books for schools, colleges and people all around the world. John aims to educate readers about the knowledge of technology geared to people who are interested in learning, and who are not familiar with computers.

Join John's fan club at http://www.jghitech.com

INDEX

INDEX

www.ingramcontent.com/pod-product-compliance
Lightning Source LLC
Chambersburg PA
CBHW060505060326
40689CB00020B/4638